Japanese
Brush Painting
in Color

by Kohei Aida

JAPAN PUBLICATIONS, INC

Published by
Japan Publications, Inc., Tokyo
Japan Publications Trading Company
1255 Howard St., San Francisco, Calif. 94103 U.S.A.
P. O. Box 5030 Tokyo International, Tokyo, Japan
Library of Congress Catalog Card No. 73-78182
ISBN-0-87040-225-0
© 1973 by Japan Publications, Inc.
First printing: September 1973
Printed in Japan by Toppan Printing Co., Ltd.

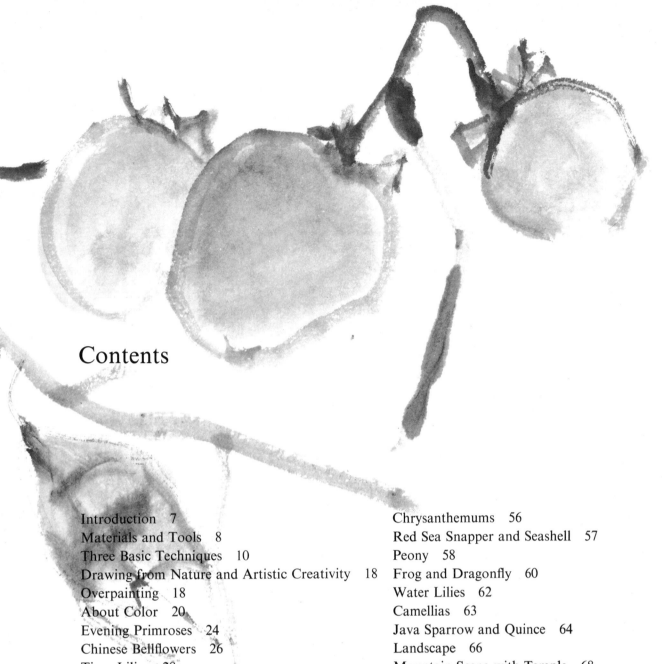

Contents

Introduction 7
Materials and Tools 8
Three Basic Techniques 10
Drawing from Nature and Artistic Creativity 18
Overpainting 18
About Color 20
Evening Primroses 24
Chinese Bellflowers 26
Tiger Lilies 28
Persimmons 30
Water Plantains and Frog 31
Herons 32
Hydrangea 34
Turtledove 36
Iris 38
Dharma 39
Bird 40
Chrysanthemums and Sparrow 42
Morning Glories 44
Cat and Narcissus 45
Mountain Scene 46
Moonlit Fishing Village 48
Praying Mantis and Crepe Myrtle 50
Squirrel 51
Pomegranate and Bluebird 52
Rose Mallow 54

Chrysanthemums 56
Red Sea Snapper and Seashell 57
Peony 58
Frog and Dragonfly 60
Water Lilies 62
Camellias 63
Java Sparrow and Quince 64
Landscape 66
Mountain Scene with Temple 68
Boulders 70
Trees 71
Sparrow and Bamboo 72
Long-armed Ape 74
Dried Lotus and Kingfisher 76
Seaside Scene 78
Oleander 80
Cow 81
Dancers at the Festival of the Lights 82
Grapes 84
Bluebird and Bitter Orange 85
Sparrow and Plum 86
Farm in the Mountains in Autumn 88
Rose 90
Wild Duck in Reeds 91
Chinese Cabbage, Yam, and Onion 92
Paintings for Reference and Study 94

Introduction

Until after World War II, all pictures belonging in the *suiboku* category of ink painting were monochrome black ink on paper or silk. Although there existed a separate school of painting employing brushwork like that used in suiboku but applying colors to pictures, it was considered part of another tradition and was not accepted as true ink painting. Among specialists, such colored paintings were referred to as *tsuketate* or *mokkotsu*. After World War II, people in many countries began to show true suiboku and in colored ink paintings. Since the basic material of both is ink, it gradually became customary abroad to group the two varieties under the name *sumi-e* (literally ink picture). Ultimately sumi-e came to be the term used even in Japan, and this development gave rise to the need for a special name to set monochrome ink painting apart from those using colors. To the present, no one name has been selected, but two have gained some currency: *saibokuga* and *bokusaiga*, both of which mean roughly pictures using both black ink and color.

Though the painting techniques employed in both suiboku and saibokuga are identical, the natures of the expressions of monochrome and colored paintings are quite different. Monochrome suiboku developed together with Zen Buddhism, which absolutely rejected color in pictures of this kind. Zen artists considered color a distractingly sensual element that entices the eye with superficial appeal but fails to lead to true spiritual depth of beauty. Monochrome paintings, on the other hand, were believed to lead to sublimity and enlightenment. For this reason, Zen priests, people in search of Buddhist truth, and artistically inclined samurai devoted themselves to black and white suiboku. It is certainly true that the aesthetics of monochrome ink paintings involves spiritual beauty. In fact, the quality of the ink itself is more conducive to the development of spiritually mystical qualities than are colored pigments. On the other hand, the world of nature is rich in colors. Knowing that it is impossible to ignore the beauties of this world, a number of artists have attempted to create a more sensually lovely, yet equally exalted, art by employing color in paintings that are nonetheless based on ink and ink-painting techniques. Shi-tao and Tessai are outstanding representatives of this group.

The color-and-ink painting methods shown in this book are all based on the ink itself. In order to preserve the beauty of ink, it is important to select the quality and quantity of color used with the greatest caution. Only if the amount and nature of the colors are suitable to the work at hand is it possible to strengthen the expressive powers of the painting and in that way expand its realm of appeal.

Materials and Tools

Brushes

The brushes used in tsuketate and mokkotsu painting, and in much painting of this kind are as follows.

Standard brushes (tsuketate or mokkotsu fude): The shafts of these brushes are longer than those of brushes for oriental calligraphy. The bristles are slightly stiff and may be either white—these are called winter bristles—or reddish—these are known as summer bristles. Both types are available in large, medium, and small sizes. Stiffer bristles are set in the core of the tip of the brush for the sake of resiliency. This means that, even after considerble use, the brush will not bend or lose its shape. Sometimes, brushes with sheep's hair bristles are sold. These are difficult to use because they are soft and lose their shape quickly. For the purposes of ink-and-color painting, it is sufficient to have one large, one small, and one medium size brush of this kind.

Horsehair burshes: Although these stiff brushes are not absolutely essential, they are useful in painting the stiffish lines needed for decayed trees or rocks and boulders. One of them is enough.

Line brushes: There are no special ink-painting brushes designed solely for lines, but it is a good idea to make one because they are very convenient. To do this, obtain a calligraphy brush used in writing fine-line characters. These are no more than one-quarter inch at the shaft near the bristles (even thinner ones are desirable if available), and the bristles are about one inch long. Reddish bristles

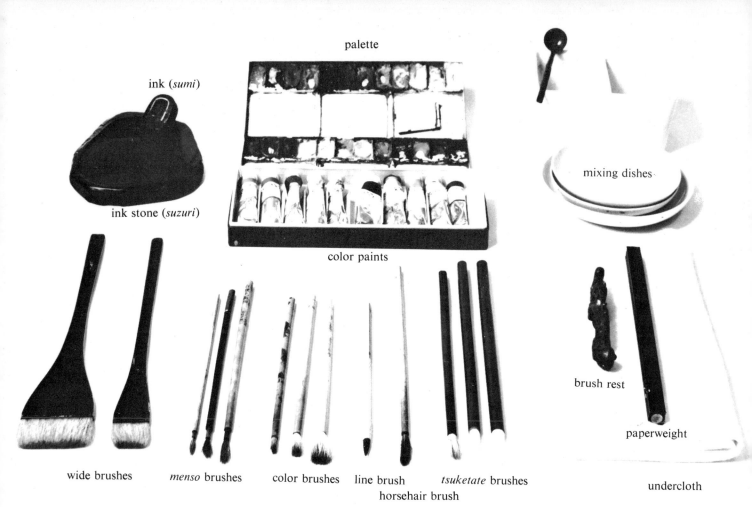

ink (*sumi*)

ink stone (*suzuri*)

palette

color paints

mixing dishes

brush rest

paperweight

wide brushes   *menso* brushes   color brushes   line brush   *tsuketate* brushes

horsehair brush

undercloth

are preferred. Stiffen the bristles and thus make them easy to use in drawing lines by impregnating them with glue and wrapping adhesive plaster around the upper half of their length. This will strengthen the tip and prevent it from becoming too thick. To complete a set of brushes to meet all line-painting requirements, you will need one line brush made as described in this section.

Color brushes: These are usually rather bushy and made of sheep's hair which will absorb large amounts of pigment. Three of them—large, medium, and small—are needed.

Menso brushes: These are used in painting long lines or linear strips. By applying pressure to them so that the entire tip comes in contact with the paper, it is possible to paint such things as the leaves of reeds with great ease. In addition, for leaf veins and vines these brushes are very convenient. A large, a medium, and a small menso brush are required.

Wide brushes: These are available in widths ranging from one inch to five inches, but for the work in this book a one-inch and five-inches brush

are sufficient. Using wide brushes and dipping one corner in the pigment and the other corner in plain water, it is possible to produce a gradually shaded effect with one stroke. This is useful in painting distant mountains and hilly land. Sometimes these brushes are charged with clear water only and drawn across the paper to which dark ink is then applied to produce a blurred effect.

Ink *(sumi)*

This is available in Japanese (*waboku*) and Chinese (*toboku*) varieties. Toboku, which is actually manufactured in China, has a strong glue base, which makes it opaque and excellent for giving the feeling of the thickness of things. Unfortunately, most of the toboku sold today is of poor quality because it contains minute, gritty crystals that scar the ink stone. I have tried to use it on a number of occasions but always with unsatisfactory results. It is better to purchase good quality Japanese ink, which comes in a brownish oil-smoke variety and in another variety with a blue cast. For the sake of a sense of color, many sumi-e painters prefer the bluish variety, but I must warn against a sham article containing indigo dye that is sometimes sold. To find out whether ink is artificially colored, follow this procedure. Paint a line with the suspect ink. A small amount of water should surround the black part of the line painted, but if that watery zone is clearly separated from the black and if it is tinged with blue, the ink is unsatisfactory. Other signs of poor-quality ink appear when the ink stick is rubbed on the ink stone. Any ink that makes a grating sound while being rubbed, that softens at the point of contact with the stone, that is sticky, or that creates an unusual quantity of bubbles is inferior. Since it is impossible to test every stick of ink purchased, it is important to select products made by reliable firms and sold by trustworthy shops.

Ink stones *(suzuri)*

Of course it is advisable to buy a good inkstone, but it is not imperative to purchase the very finest and most famous varieties. Japanese stones sold under the name *Amabata Shinseki*, for instance, are perfectly adequate. They are not too soft, and ink rubbed on them is smooth. Still, within this brand, there are grades of excellence; one must be careful to select the best. There are a number of good brands in addition to this one. Generally a rectangular ink stone is best, though some of the expensive ones made from natural stones are irregular in shape.

Paper

Suitable papers are of the following varieties: *Gasenshi, Nisoshi, Gyokubansen, Toshi, Gahoshi,* and ordinary *Washi*, or Japanese paper.

Gasenshi: This Chinese paper smears and tears easily. It is not recommended for use by beginners. It's smearing and blotting characteristic mean that, when it is wet, it is impossible to overpaint. But there is a way of avoiding this difficulty. If tube Chinese white is mixed with the ink and the areas painted with this material allowed to dry, overpainting becomes possible. This same method is employed with other papers that smear and blot easily, but I shall talk about this point more in detail later.

Gyokubansen: Since this paper has extremely high powers of absorption, it is often impossible to connect painted ink lines satisfactorily. Consequently, achieving the desired even color requires great skill and familiarity with the nature of the paper. Furthermore, although lines painted black on this paper look a rich black when they are wet, they dry to a thinnish, sharp tone. One then naturally wants to overpaint, but overpainted lines look too dark because the original strokes regain their original blackness. All in all, it is difficult to estimate the effects Gyokubansen paper will produce. This is true of all thick papers; therefore, in working with them, one must always attempt to take into consideration the effects that a backing will have on the color of the ink. Gyokubansen and Asagami (see below) are too expensive for the trial paintings of students in their early stages of development.

Washi: Produced in the same way as papers for sliding partitions (*shoji*) and other Japanese papers, Asagami is especially good for landscapes because brush marks are not clearly left on it. This makes overpainting possible. From the standpoint of ink application, however, it is less satisfactory since the boundaries between shaded areas tend to blur when made on this paper. Nonetheless, it is often used for large or complicated pictures.

Nisoshi: Made of two sheets of Gasenshi pasted together, this paper is widely used because it blots less noticeably, does not show brush marks, and allows moderate overpainting.

Toshi: The paper sold today as *Niban Toshi*, is inferior. Nonetheless, because it is inexpensive, has good blotting characteristics, and permits overpainting, it is difficult to discard. Because of low cost it is recommended to beginners.

Shoji Paper and other Japanese Papers: All of the purely Japanese papers, including the kind used to fill the sliding paper panels in Japanese windows are good for practice and for works of art because they produce handsome ink colors, permit overpainting, and have good blotting characteristics. This paper is available in a bleached white and in an unbleached reddish color. Most Japanese papers are inexpensive.

Shikishi: This paper is available in several sizes and in two types: *Wagasen* and *Hongasen*, the latter of which produce the lovelier ink colors and has better blotting qualities. In general, the touch of these papers to the brush is somewhat stiff.

9

Paperweight

A paperweight is essential to hold the paper in place during painting. Since brush strokes are sometimes made with considerable force, the weight must be heavy enough to prevent the paper's moving. On the other hand, it must not be so long that it becomes a hindrance.

Undercloth

This too is essential because, if one attempts to paint without it, ink will seep through the paper, not only spoiling whatever lies under it, but also staining the back of the picture and possibly ruining what might have been a fine work. The undercloth may be wool or felt, but it must be white. Japanese shops specializing in calligraphy or ink-painting equipment sell cloths cut to suitable sizes, but it is possible to make one out of available materials.

Containers for washing brushes

These may be plastic or porcelain and either round or rectangular in shape, but for the sake of convenience they ought to be large.

Ink dishes

Excellent ink dishes are made in sets for use in Japanese-style paintings. For ink-and-color work, select one dish about five inches in diameter for ink and four or five about three inches in diameter for color pigments.

Color paints

Colors for Japanese-style paintings and for color-and-ink work have recently been put on sale in convenient sets of tubes from which one may squeeze out only the amount needed. Old-fashioned porcelain containers of pigments too are still available. And if you live in a region where neither of the Japanese-style color paints is available, tubes of watercolor paints are suitable.

Charcoal

This is used to sketch in the general composition of pictures. It must be of the soft, Japanese kind that erases easily and completely. This charcoal is available in speciality stores.

Absorbent cotton

A small amount of absorbent cotton must be used to remove charcoal lines from the paper.

Brush rest

This is necessary because putting the ink or color brushes down carelessly soils the working area and might ruin a picture.

Care of Equipment

Brushes: After using them, carefully wash all brushes, blot moisture from them with waste paper, and align their bristles carefully. Then wrap and put them in a container. Since oil stains spoil not only brushes but also all other ink-painting equipment, never wash brushes in the kitchen where such contamination is likely to occur.

Containers for ink and paints and for washing brushes: Once again, do not wash these together with food utensils because, treated in that way, they may become contaminated with oil. If these containers are oily—because of the nature of procelain surfaces, oil tends to adhere to them—they will contaminate the brushes, which will soon split at the tips and become unusable. As an added precaution, always wipe containers with paper just before using them.

Ink stone: Always wash ink stones after each use: ink must not be allowed to remain on them.

Three Basic Techniques

1. Charging the Brush

The shadings possible by mixing ink with water are more distinctive and lovelier than anything possible with other pigments. This beauty has a deeply spiritual quality that, associated with the long history of oriental calligraphy and ink painting, surpasses the color of the ink itself. Although the standard gradations of ink in paintings are dark, medium, and light, when actually applied to paper, ink produces many subtle shadings resulting in a profound loveliness. The exact effects of these shadings are often difficult to forecast. The method of grading intensity of color in the brush is exactly the same no matter whether the medium is ink or colored pigments. In almost 80 percent of all lines and surfaces painted, this gradation of intensity—called *notan* in Japanese—is employed. But at this point, I must interject a word about technique as such.

Technique is always only a method to achieve an expressive end. That is to say, the most important thing in painting must be the subjective views and emotions of the painter. If an artist feels that it would be more effective to abandon traditional gradation methods and to use overpaintings of three separate intensities of ink, he must be allowed to try this technique. In other words, artists are obliged to adopt a free approach to the use of ink in order to be able to express emotions frankly and accurately. I shall now explain the method of grading the shades of ink in the brush, but I must say that the artist is by no means constrained to use this method in all cases.

1. First fill the well of the stone with clear water and prepare liquid ink by rubbing the ink stick on the ink stone. Draw the dark liquid ink from the well to the mound (hill) of the stone then push it toward the well again. This will enable you to pre-

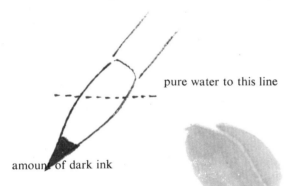

pure water to this line

amount of dark ink

intensity of light ink

vent the ink from accumulating in excess on the mound and will also provide adequate ink that will not dry out immediately. If you are using a new brush, wash it to remove the sizing and to soften the bristles. Fill the brush with clear water and transfer its contents to the ink dish by rubbing the brush three or four times against the rim.

2. Dip the tip of the brush into the dark ink of the ink stone. The ink must extend to about one-quarter of an inch from the tip of the brush (see drawing below). Now mix this ink with the water in the dish to produce a pale ink-water solution. In mixing, do not allow the pale ink to fill the entire brush; that is, the area at the base of the bristles must remain filled with clear water. This can be done easily by holding the brush at about a forty-

A

B

C

five-degree angle and mixing the solution with one side of the brush only.

Particles of oily substances present in the air sometimes cause trouble at this stage by mixing with the ink solution and making it streaky and uneven. If this happens, it is necessary to discard the contents of the dish, wipe it thoroughly with a cloth or paper towel, and start over again.

3. Next open the bristles and flatten the brush by making wide zigzag strokes over the surface of the dish. Begin at the side of the dish away from you and repeat the process two or three times (Fig. A).

Exert light pressure on the brush as you make the zigzag strokes.

4. It is now necessary to remove excess pale ink solution from the bristles. Put the brush in a horizontal position by turning your wrist to the right (Fig. B). Rest the shaft of the brush on the edge of the dish at a point about an inch from the base of the bristles. Then, with swift motions draw the bristles over the rim of the dish. This is best accomplished by moving the wrist outward. Apply light pressure to the brush and repeat the movement three times (Fig. C).

D

E

H

F

5. To remove pale ink from the other side of the brush, leave the three fingers supporting the shaft in the same position, but turn the brush over by drawing your thumb forward. The position seems somewhat awkward at first, but you will soon become accustomed to it. Applying light pressure; repeat three times (Figs. D and E).

6. The amount of pale ink in the brush will now be neither too great nor too small. Return the brush to its original position by simply thrusting your thumb forward. It is now necessary to adjust

G

I

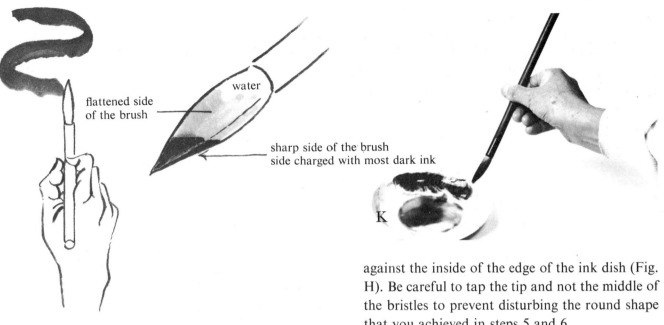

flattened side
of the brush

water

sharp side of the brush
side charged with most dark ink

K

J

the shape of the bristles, which have been disorder-ed in the preceding two steps. Resting the shaft of the brush on the edge of the ink dish, draw the bristles across the rim lightly. No pressure need be applied since it is not necessary to remove liquid at this stage (Figs. F and G).

7. In step 6, the bristles will have been straight-ened, but the tip of the brush remains flared. Correct this by lightly tapping both sides of the tip

against the inside of the edge of the ink dish (Fig. H). Be careful to tap the tip and not the middle of the bristles to prevent disturbing the round shape that you achieved in steps 5 and 6.

8. You must now take further dark ink from the inkstone. If the flat part of the stone has dried, draw some ink from the well. Never dip the brush directly into the well. Ink is not taken from the stone with the flattened tip, but with one side. Holding the brush at forty-five degrees increases the area of contact of bristles with the inkstone (see drawing in upper left corner of p. 13 and Fig. I).

9. At this point, the areas of pale and dark ink are clearly defined: there is no zone of medium ink intensity. But it is necessary to create one by fol-lowing this procedure. With the side containing the dark ink down, press the bristles against the sloping right inner side of the dish. Pulling the brush toward you, make a zigzag line about two inches long. Repeat this process, beginning at a point about two-thirds of the way from the start of the first zigzag. This will blend the dark and light ink to form an intermediary zone of medium intensity and will prevent the ink from coloring the pure water at the base of the bristles (Fig. J).

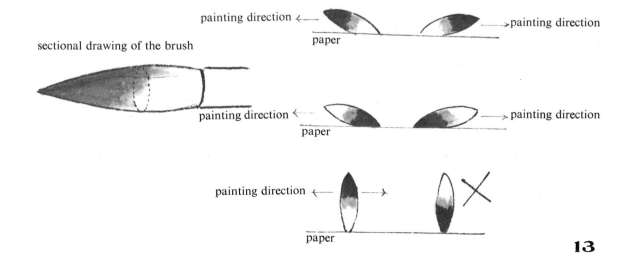

sectional drawing of the brush

painting direction ←—   —→ painting direction
paper

painting direction ←—   —→ painting direction
paper

painting direction ←   →
paper

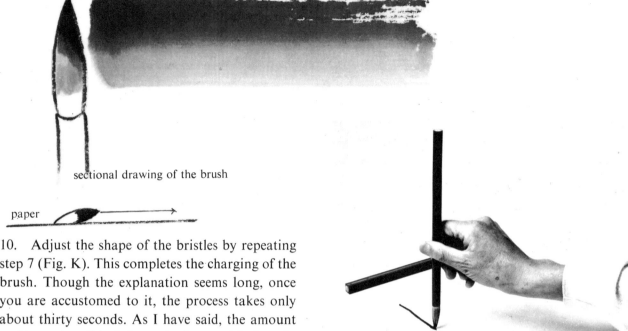

sectional drawing of the brush

paper

10. Adjust the shape of the bristles by repeating step 7 (Fig. K). This completes the charging of the brush. Though the explanation seems long, once you are accustomed to it, the process takes only about thirty seconds. As I have said, the amount and intensity of the ink required vary with the subject of the picture, but the charging process is invariable.

It is now almost time to put the brush to paper, but before doing so, it is imperative to observe one inviolable rule: only the side of the brush with the lesser amount of ink must touch the paper. The side with the dark ink must always be turned either up or to one side. Consequently, after charging the brush, turn it so that the darker side is upper. I shall explain the correct ways to use the brush in the following section, but at this point, draw a horizontal line with the brush just charged with three shades of ink. Next, turn the brush so that the dark side is not parallel with the paper, but is raised lightly from it, and make a broad line to the right. (see drawing on p. 13). If the medium ink zone is approximately like the one in the illustration, the brush has been correctly filled, and the line is well drawn. But as the brush is used, this zone may become softer. In addition, according to the subject being painted, it is sometimes desirable to avoid very vague modulations among the shaded zones.

Since, during actual painting, the brush must be refilled and adjusted many times, the pale ink in the dish will darken, or the amount of water will become excessive. When this happens, you must discard the contents of the dish and begin again. Always maintain about one brushful of pale ink solution in the dish.

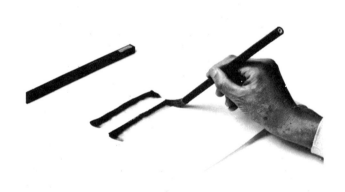

2. Three Brushstrokes

To the traditional straight stroke and side stroke of oriental calligraphy ink painting adds a half-side stroke.

1. Straight stroke: Used mostly for linear work, this stroke is characterized by the fact that the axis of the brush travels through a plane perpendicular to the line being drawn; that is, the brush must not lean to the left or the right. Generally the brush is held in a perfectly vertical position, as seen in Fig. 1. But sometimes the size of the paper or the position in which one must work makes this impossible. In short, though conditions sometimes require that the brush be tilted forward or backward, in this stroke it is never inclined to the sides: lines

drawn with the brush tilted left or right become side strokes.

2. Side strokes: As the name indicates, this stroke moves right or left. The brush is held at a ninety-degree angle to the direction in which the stroke is made. Sometimes, however, the angle is decreased to make strokes almost the full width of the tip of the brush or increased to make narrower strokes. In contrast to the procedure used in the straight stroke, for which the brush must remain perpendicular to the direction of movement, in the side stroke, this angle may be varied. The most widely used way of holding the brush for ink painting is as shown in Fig. 3. The brush is pointed

forward, and the palm of the hand is turned forward. There are two other grips: one in which the tip of the brush is turned to point toward the painter and one in which the back of the hand is held upward. The latter is used in calligraphy (Fig. 2). These two ways, however, are rarely used in ink painting because they restrict the movement of the brush.

The sample strokes below were all made with the brush held in the position shown in Figs. 2 and 3. The angle between the brush and the paper increases in numerical order from the stroke in the lower left to that in the lower right. These illustrations show that side strokes can be made in many directions and at many angles.

In strokes 1 through 3, the shaft of the brush points forward; in stroke 4, the brush is held on a horizontal line; and in strokes 5 through 7, the tip of the brush points forward. In all of the strokes, however, the hand is held with the inner side of the palm turned forward. Strokes accompanied by dotted-line drawings of brushes might be executed with the calligraphy method, in which the back of the hand is turned upward.

Stroke 1 is useful for painting the thick trunks of trees and stroke 7 for thin lines. Stroke 6 was devised for wide monochrome areas like those used

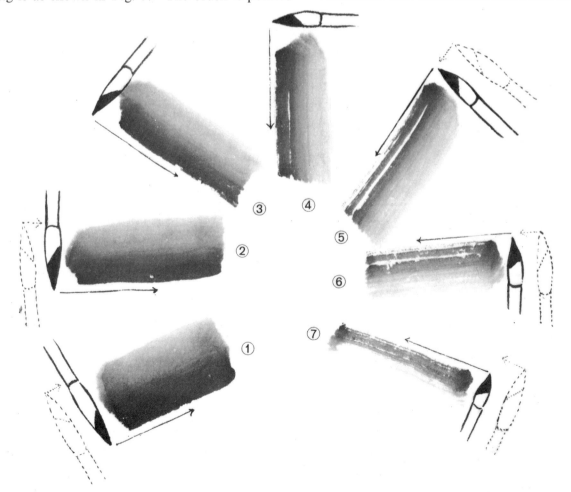

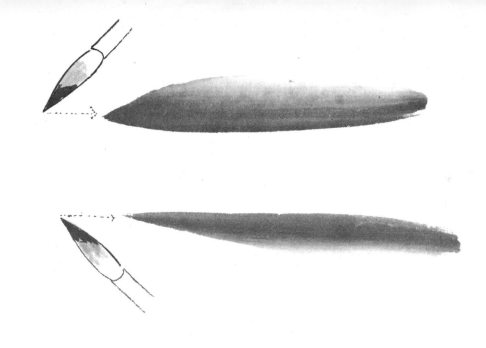

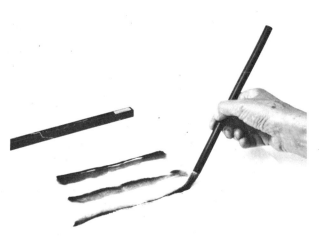

in representing distant mountains. Because of the way the brush is charged, the part of the stroke corresponding to the tip of the bristles is always dark. The arrows indicate that all of the strokes were made by drawing the brush forward, but if the person painting feels no discomfort in doing so, they might just as easily be made in the reverse direction.

3. **Half-side stroke:** These strokes are made by holding the brush at a right or left forty-five degree angle to the paper. Though not employed often, the stroke is convenient for painting things that start with narrow lines and gradually thicken, like vine leaves or bird plumage. The method of execution is the same as that used in the side stroke.

3. Arm and Brush Movement

Almost all ink paintings employ an arm and brush movement called *kenwan-sokuhitsu*, which means a side-stroke of the brush made with the arm moving free in the air above the paper. This stroke produces lines that are fluid and that have no clearly demarcated points where the motion seems to come to a complete stop. The brush is held and moved as explained in the section on the side stroke. The distinctive feature of this special technique is that the movement of the arm and brush begins in the air about two or three inches to the side of the place where the brush actually comes into contact with the paper and continues into the air for a few inches after the brush has left the paper. The motions are neither especially fast nor especially slow. Once you have mastered the idea of the stroke, you will find it easy, although at first achieving the correct finish may cause some trouble. It is important to grip the brush lightly and to move the whole arm. As the drawing above shows, side strokes made with this kind of movement produce almost straight lines that thicken with a rounded quality. The roundness results from the fact that the thick part of the line is made with the thick part of the brush tip. If the lines you make with this technique resemble willow leaves or the shapes of small fish, they have been properly drawn. Correctly used, this technique can produce beautiful tonal gradations even in slender lines. In addition, wide areas can be filled with beautifully shaded ink with only a few brush strokes. A few examples of these strokes used in simple compositions appear on p. 17.

The orchid blossom is made of five slender strokes. The camellia leaf below it is a combination of two broad strokes. The brush was lifted sharply from the paper to form the typical straight point

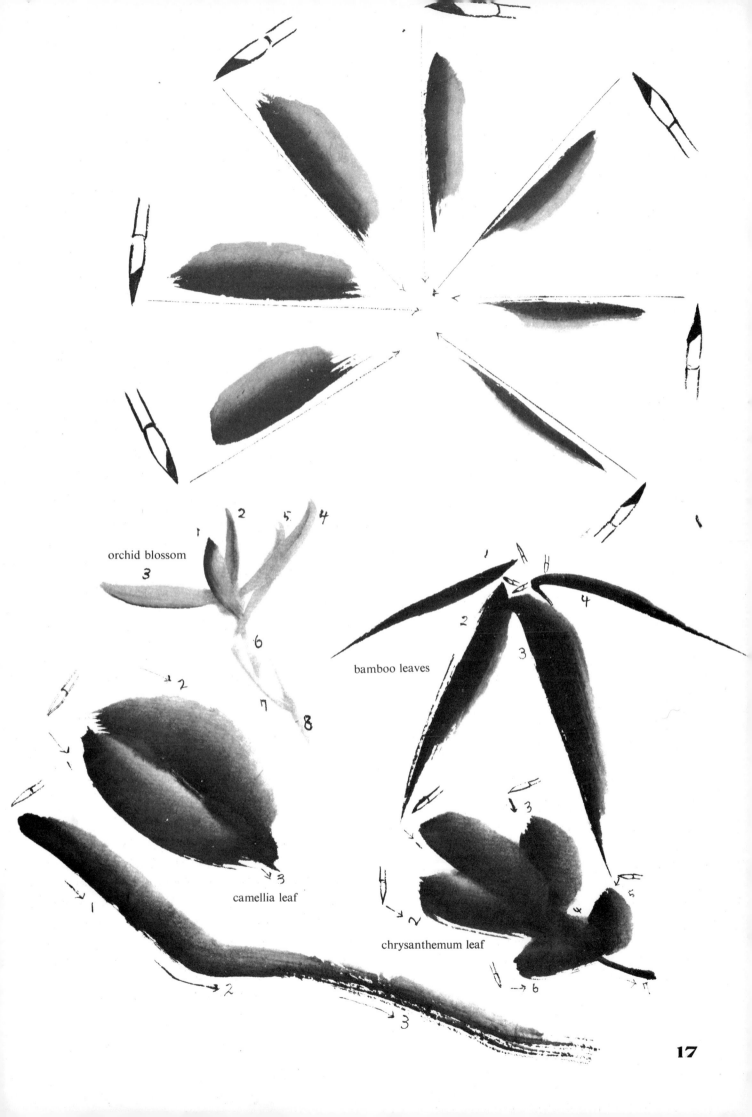

orchid blossom

bamboo leaves

camellia leaf

chrysanthemum leaf

at one end of the leaf. To make the bamboo leaves, extra pressure was applied at the beginning of each stroke, which was then extended for a considerable length. Six of these side strokes were used to paint the chrysanthemum leaf, and a straight stroke was added for the stem. The branch at the bottom of the page is actually made of three of these strokes, but because of the nature of the brushwork the junctions among the parts are not apparent.

The range of applications of the kenwan-soku-hitsu stroke is so extensive that unless you master it through repeated practice, success in ink painting is impossible.

Drawing from Nature and Artistic Creativity

Once you have mastered the basic techniques and have attained a certain proficiency in producing versions of the models presented in this book, you will be ready to start painting your own pictures of plants, animals, and landscapes. The first step in developing the ability to do this successfully is drawing from nature, which is of the greatest importance because it enables one to understand the true shapes of all kinds of objects. You must practice this kind of work diligently and often; and in doing so, you must take care that your drawings are accurate. Drawing from nature in itself, however, does not produce a work of art.

I always tell my students that unless half of a picture is fictitious it will have no true value. Though the word *fictitious* may seem to have unattractive connotations, I mean only that a work of art must be something different from pure nature copying. In other words, a copy of a natural object or scene, no matter how skillfully executed and accurate, represents nothing but the exteriors of those things and has little artistic expression. In art, spiritual impact is more important than technique. Even if he is not immediately conscious of trying to produce a specific impact, however, the painter must establish a plan and devise ways to give expression to his own feelings. Furthermore, he must have the will to realize those plans. For example, when painting a flower, the artist must perceive the personality of the subject, the nature of the environment in which the flower exists, the sense of the time of year in which it blooms, and something of the life force of the plant. Small, simple flowers require a gentle, subtle painting approach, whereas the magnificence of something like the peony demands emphasis on richness.

A man who sits impassively smoking a cigarette and feeling nothing as he observes a natural scene, will never give that scenery moving artistic representation. One must pour all of one's attention into the scene, become one with the very special world embodying the particular view, and then, experiencing a kind of electrical charge running up one's spine, seize the image of the moment and put it on paper. I often explain this to my students. When some of them claim that they have never experienced anything like the feeling I describe, I tell them that they must try to understand nature as the catalyst that inspires both images and emotions in the artist.

On the other hand, though abundant imagination and emotional sensitivity are necessary, it is possible to remove oneself so far from the actual world of nature, that one falls into the trap of becoming self-satisfied. As long as the kind of art in question is representational, it must be true to the mood, personality, and life force of nature. Artists in this realm must strive for a harmonious blend of accurate representation and emotion, or of objectivity and subjectivity.

Receptivity to emotion and expression differs with the individual, as do motives and methods of giving these things artistic realization. Some people are born with well-developed artistic sensibilities, but in many cases, the awakening to beauty is gradual. Then suddenly, at a certain moment, the individual finds that he is able to produce outstanding works.

In summary, then, the artist must first realize the difference between accurate representation and artistic expression. In drawing from nature, he must always keep the idea of expression in mind. Once the plan for expressing the blend of fact and fiction that the picture will become has matured in his mind, the artist proceeds to eliminate excess things that distract from his aim and to emphasize the elements that are the heart of the expression that he is striving to realize. The artist, by employing a certain amount of fiction, arrives at something closer to truth than the real object itself.

Overpainting

Contrary to the commonly held idea among beginners, ink painting is not a matter of quick strokes drawn and never retouched. As a matter of fact, in ink paintings of all sizes, overpainting is widely employed. Exact methods are difficult to establish and hard to explain since the techniques employed vary with the nature of the paper and with the size of the picture. Furthermore the amount of time required for the first ink strokes to dry differs according to the absorbent qualities of the paper. For instance, very thin papers that blot easily do not permit overpainting. Sometimes Chinese white is added to the ink used with such papers to retard blotting. Chinese white to some extent spoils the color of the ink and produces opaque areas in the paper. Still, the opaque areas in themselves often vary the depth of the picture and thereby heighten its interest. Chinese artists have frequently resorted to this method. Another method used with papers that blot readily is to paint once, allow the ink to dry, paint again, dry the second coat, and paint once again. When dried, the fish glue used in the ink creates a surface that retards blotting.

As a rule, no more than three applications of ink are made because, this does not dull or sully the appearance of the paper. In addition, the area covered by the first overpainting and the amount of ink used are smaller than those of the original strokes. The area of the second overpainting is smaller still. To use the same amount and to cover the same area each time reduces the ink color to a dull black and produces a flat area that gives no sense of space (see Fig. A).

No matter how small the area covered, it is necessary to manifest all three ink colors—light, medium, and dark—and to blend them in a soft, yet fresh, way. The landscape on p. 46 shows the kind of gradations and harmony that are needed. It is usually unadvisable, however, to apply a coat of pale ink, dry it, then add medium and dry that, and finally add dark. This method does not allow the color zones to blend gently; furthermore it produces overly distinct lines and visible brushmarks. Always charge the brush with three colors as outlined in the preceding section, and then apply it to the area of pale ink already on the paper.

In charging the brush for overpainting, pay very close attention to the quantity of water (or pale ink) taken into the bristles. It must be somewhat less than is used for ordinary painting so that when the first overpaint layer is applied to the pale ink on the paper, water will not extend beyond the boundaries of the painted zone. This necessitates limiting the amount of pure dark ink taken from the ink stone. If the paper is not one that blots readily, the second overpainting may be done with the same brush while the first overpainting is still wet. If the paper blots easily, each coat must be dried before the next is added. The area of the first overpainting must be about 80 percent of the first coat. That of the second overpainting is still smaller since it will become the darkest part, the area that draws the composition together.

I must add an important warning. Correct effective overpainting depends on experience gained as a result of practice and mistakes understood and corrected. The beginner cannot expect to do it well the first time on the basis of no more than having read an explanation like the one offered here.

The outline in the preceding paragraphs pertains to overpainting on papers that absorb and blot readily. I shall now offer a few words on the process for overpainting with less absorbent papers. First, charge the brush with three tones according to the standard procedure. Then take a small amount of dark ink from the stone on the tip of the brush. Adjust this by lightly stroking the bristles on the ink dish. In this way you will produce a somewhat darker middle tone of ink and a somewhat weaker dark zone.

Using a brush charged in this way, begin by painting the major parts of the composition and move to the subordinate parts as the ink in the bristles becomes weaker and paler. When replenishing the supply of ink in the brush, always keep this process in mind so that you do not make the mistake of creating several parts with the same ink tones and strengths. After painting the entire picture with a first coat, add another to darken the parts requiring intensification. As I have said, the area of the second coat is smaller than that of the first. It does not always happen that you achieve

Overpainting Chart A

1. The paper used is thin and highly absorbent. A small amount of white was added to a pale ink solution. After the strokes were made, they were allowed to dry.

2. Paper and procedures are the same as those used in Fig. 1.

3. The first overpainting is made on top of the strokes prepared in step 1 above. The brush used was charged with graded pale and medium ink, and the strokes were allowed to dry completely. Ink was applied over the entire surface.

4. The brush was charged as in Fig. 3, but only about half of the original area was overpainted.

5. The brush was charged with pale, medium, and dark ink; and overpainting was applied over the entire area. Consequently, the painted zone is rendered dull and flat.

6. The brush was charged as in Fig. 5, but overpainting was used in still less of the total area than in Fig. 4. Gradually reducing the area painted results in variation and a sense of depth. No matter how small the area painted, you must strive to achieve this effect.

Overpainting Chart B

The upper and lower versions of the leaves were painted on two different kinds of paper, both of which have moderate absorption characteristics. The brush was charged with pale, medium, and dark ink in the usual fashion. Beginning with the darkest leaves, paint the entire set once with the same brush. Recharging the brush correctly, overpaint. Allow the overpainting to dry (although with certain absorbent paper, drying is not necessary).

When using paper with low absorption qualities, allowing the undercoat to dry before applying medium and dark ink, results in dark overpaint areas that are very conspicuous when the entire picture is dry. To prevent this, I first use a brush charged with pale and a light medium ink from which I press most of the moisture so that the brush does not wet, but more or less grazes, the surface of the paper. For the overpainting I use a brush charged with pale, medium, and dark ink. This, of course, is not the only method possible, but I find that it produces a pleasingly soft, well-blended appearance.

the tonal gradation and distribution you want on the first coat. In fact, after the first coat is complete, it often happens that darkness is lacking in some areas where it is needed and that certain places are too dark as a consequence of brush recharging. In applying the second coat, too, begin with the most important parts of the picture and move gradually to the subordinate ones. Even following this procedure does not guarantee satisfactory results all the time (see Fig. B).

Even with papers of low absorption and blotting characteristics, overpainting is usually limited to two coats, and each is dried before the other is applied. By and large, the second coat applied throughout the picture will take care of most of the tonal gradation. It will then remain only to add certain points for emphasis or for the sake of binding the composition together. In the second overpainting, there may be places where brush marks will make no difference to the success of the work, but there will also be those where traces of the brush or areas where the dark ink does not blend well with its surroundings detract from the picture. To prevent such unpleasant phenomena, follow this procedure. Before adding dark ink to the tip of the brush, firmly squeeze out most of the moisture from the bristles already charged with light and medium ink. Pass this brush over the paper in a grazing fashion leaving some moist and some completely dry zones. Then overpaint with dark and medium ink. The tones will blend gently, and no distinctly delineated dark spots will form.

The darkest spots that are the key point of the picture must be painted with the first strokes applied to clean paper and not put off till last. After making these strokes, proceed to the general work of the painting.

About Color

For color ink paintings, pale, transparent paints are used. These may be of the oriental variety called *gansai,* new paints designed for traditional Japanese-style pictures, or the ordinary watercolors found throughout the world. Unless the color pigments are greatly thinned, the resulting picture will have the coarse, cheap look of commercial postures. Prussian blue and ultramarine require special attention to thinning, for, if too intense, they can destroy the distinct beauty of the black

ink itself. Red ochre too must be greatly thinned. It is possible to mix as many as three pigments, but no more. And, when adding the third pigment, you must use only one-third or one-fourth the amount of the other two. Color pigments are mixed in dishes according to the procedure outlined for preparing ink. Do not overmix the colors because this can spoil their effectiveness. The greens available in paint sets do not resemble the natural colors of leaves and plants. Therefore, a more natural appearance can be obtained by mixing watercolor dark yellow and Prussian blue.

It is inadvisable to mix certain pairs of colors, which in combination produce an unpleasing, dirty effect. For example, vermilion may be mixed successfully with the warm colors—yellows, reds, or browns—but must not be combined with the cool blues or greens. Similarly, red must not be mixed with green, blue-purple with yellow, or orange with blue. In general, do not mix complementary colors, but use them in adjacent areas so that they can mutually accent each other to produce an attractive harmony. An example of this kind of color use is the addition of a red temple building to a green mountain scene. Even without the building, however, a touch of red here and there in a total green composition intensifies the verdure. Remember that colors have distinctive personalities calling for distinctive treatments. For instance, since the warm reds, yellows and oranges tend to be conspicuous, they must be applied in small quantities. The cool blues, greens, and purples, on the other hand, are retiring tones that can be applied with a more generous hand.

I must repeat the admonition that color pigments must be greatly thinned. If a certain color area in a painting seems insufficiently intense, a sense of thickness and depth as well as color clarity can be achieved by waiting until the color paint dries and then overpainting as seems necessary.

Mixing Colors and Charging Brushes
As I have said, the method for mixing color and charging the brush with color is exactly the same as that used in dealing with ink. First prepare a pale color solution in the dish, make four or five zigzag motions with the tip of the brush to charge it with the pale ink; take care that the part of the bristles at the base remains filled with nothing but clear water. Then take the needed amount of dark pig-

ment on the tip of the same brush. Do not take the paint directly from the tube; instead squeeze out a small amount in a convenient receptacle. It is possible, of course, to squeeze out larger quantities of paint on a palette for later use, but this practice is unwise. The paint naturally dries out and requires a certain amount of scrubbing with the brush to soften. This in turn overmixes the paint in the brush. When overmixed pigments are applied to paper, their characteristics have already been been altered to the extent that they will not result in the effect planned. Generally make no more than four or five—at the very most five or six—zigzag strokes to mix paints. Apply the color-charged brush to the paper with a side stroke, taking care to see that one side of the stroke is softer and more blurred than the other. Beautiful color work cannot be expected if both sides of the stroke are equally well defined. If this kind of brushwork is always employed, interesting shading can be achieved in the smallest areas and with the palest colors. The bee in the picture of an oleander on p. 80 illustrates my meaning. If the wings and body of the insect had been painted with a flat color of uniform intensity, they would have had no sense of softness and roundness.

Two special color-application techniques that occur occasionally in the directions and samples in this book require explanation. 1. Sometimes, for special effect, a small amount of pure color within a surrounding area of another color or tone is desirable. In such cases, charge the brush with the basic color first. Next dip the tip of the brush in a very small amount of the color needed to produce the desired effect. Without mixing, apply the brush directly to the paper. 2. Although I have said that overmixing is generally bad, in rare cases somewhat more mixing with the brush is important. This should be done by making as many as eight small zigzag motions with the brush in the mixing dish. Instances requiring this kind of mixing will be clearly indicated.

A twelve-color set of watercolors will be adequate to the needs of all the pictures shown in this book, though it might be advisable to provide yourself with larger tubes of light yellow, burnt sienna, cobalt, and Chinese white. If you can obtain Japanese paints, you might complement your set of ordinary water colors with tubes of light cobalt blue (*bakuroku*), or *bakugunsho*) and indigo (*ai*). Generally watercolors are sold by the tube as well as by the set. This enables one to replace colors that have been exhausted without going to the expense of purchasing a full complement of colors. Watercolors have the decided disadvantage of hardening when exposed to air. Once they have set in this way, it is difficult to dissolve them successfully with the bristles of the brush. In such instances, one must soften them with wet fingers, a messy and inconvenient practice.

Evening Primroses

This pictures is an example of the generally applied color-ink-painting technique of using no outlines but employing instead areas of ink or pigment that suggest the form of the subject. To these areas, shading and lines, where needed, are added

after the basic forms are painted. Using a tsuketate brush charged with very pale yellow watercolor, paint the general forms of the flowers. While the yellow is still wet, add a minimum of shadow with very pale ink. For the shading, a line or tsuketate brush is suitable.

The shading lines will be stiff and unattractive unless (1) the tip of the brush is charged so that the pale ink and pure water areas are correctly preserved, (2) most of the moisture has been pressed from the bristles.

Allow the flowers to become about half dry before applying their outlines. While waiting, paint the buds. For this step, select a line brush, preferably one you have made yourself. Charge it first with the yellow used in the flowers then with pale and medium ink in that order. Blend these pigments in the bristles by making five or six zigzag strokes on mixing dish. After painting the buds, add the stem immediately below the flowers. Return to the buds and give each a calyx. By this time the flowers should be dry. To paint their outlines, wash the brush used for the stem and buds. Charge it with pale and medium ink and press out most of the moisture.

Chinese Bellflowers

The picture is painted in the following order:
flowers, buds, stems, leaves, grasses, insect. First
wash a medium tsuketate brush. Thin some light
cobalt blue till it is very pale and charge the brush
to about three-quarters full with it. Press most of
the liquid from the bristles. Next charge the same
brush about half full of darker cobalt blue and dip
just the tip in a very small quantity of carmine or

crimson lake. Blend these lightly by making two or three zigzag strokes across the surface of the mixing dish. Unless you follow this procedure, the petals will not have a pleasantly soft appearance. The petals require the kenwan-sokuhitsu brush strokes; that is, the brush moves through the air for one or two inches before coming into contact with the paper. When painting the buds, increase the amount of carmine red in the brush slightly to produce a purplish tone that contrasts pleasingly with the petals.

Select either large menso brush or a tsuketate brush for the stems. After charging it, press most of the moisture from the bristles. Begin the leaves by painting the large, dark one in the center, move upward to the smaller ones, and finally downward to the older, lighter colored leaves at the base of the stem. The leaves, too, must be painted with strokes that begin with the brush traveling through the air for one or two inches before touching the paper.

Tiger Lilies

Mix carmine and vermilion to achieve the desired color. Charge the brush first with pale then the tip only with darker color. Blend by making four or five zigzag strokes on the mixing dish. This version of the tiger lily is impressionistic. Without worrying too much about details, allow your brush to move freely to generate a mood suited to the flowers. The shapes will vary from the natural forms of the blossoms, but this in itself contributes a kind of interest. When all of the flowers have been painted, examine the composition with an eye to balance of strong and weak parts; add dark color where needed to improve this balance.

In painting the stems, the leaves, and the stamens of the flowers, it is not necessary to follow the order indicated by the numbers in the model. The important thing is to keep in mind at all times the balance among the strong and weak elements Overpainting may be used to achieve variety where it is needed.

29

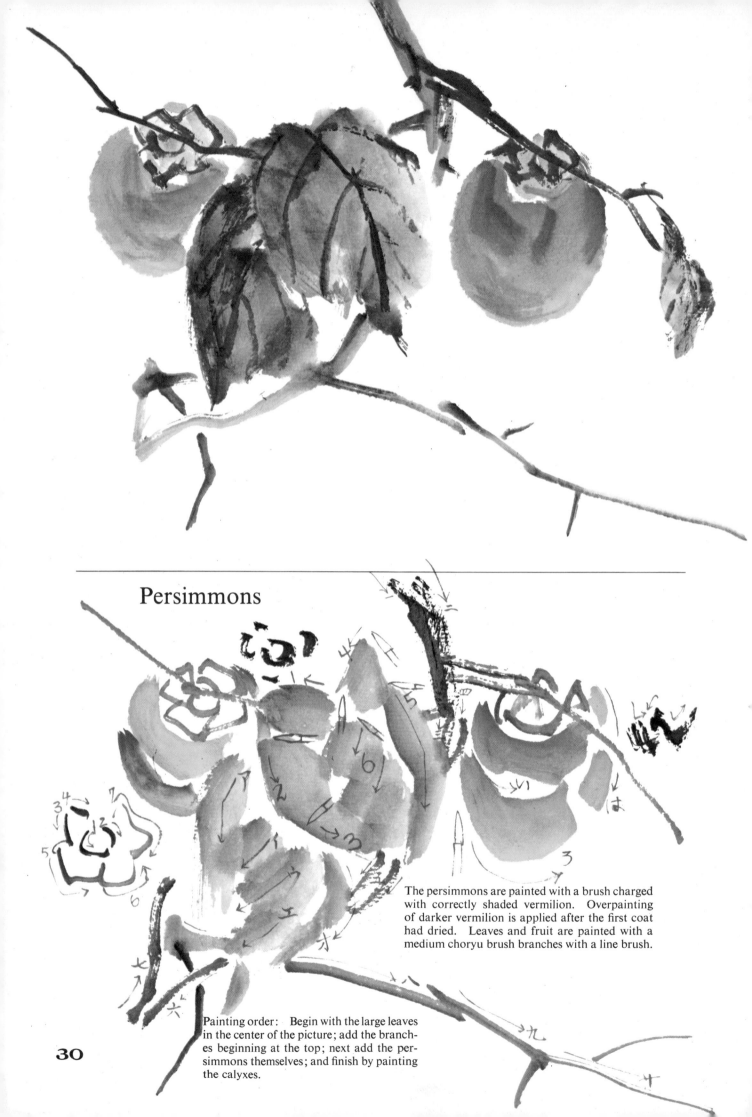

Persimmons

The persimmons are painted with a brush charged with correctly shaded vermilion. Overpainting of darker vermilion is applied after the first coat had dried. Leaves and fruit are painted with a medium choryu brush branches with a line brush.

Painting order: Begin with the large leaves in the center of the picture; add the branches beginning at the top; next add the persimmons themselves; and finish by painting the calyxes.

Water Plantains and Frog

The frog is painted first, then the plantain leaves. Use either a small line brush or small choryu brush for the frog.

The color of the frog body is obtained by mixing yellow with dark chrome green.

31

Herons

In paintings of all kinds, careful selection of the type and size of the brush greatly affects both the amount of labor that must be expended and the effect of the finished picture. Never make the mistake of thinking that skillful wielding of only one kind of brush will produce all the necessary ink-painting effects and moods. For this picture, you will require a small brush and a line brush that you have made yourself.

Press a small tsuketate brush charged with pale ink until it is fairly dry. Dip the tip of the bristles in dark ink. Holding it at an angle for a side stroke, begin by painting the initial strokes for the birds' bodies. The brush must be dry enough and must only graze the surface of the paper or the succeeding strokes will blur and fail to produce the desired effects. Steps 5 through 8 are made with a slightly darker ink. Now, selecting a line brush, paint the heads and beaks in the numerical order shown in the model. It is especially important that the brush be charged with pale, medium, and dark ink in the prescribed manner. If you are lax in this procedure, the various parts of the heads and beaks will not blend, but will remain isolated entities producing a rigid, unpleasing appearance. The same thing is true of the brush employed in painting the tails. Wash the brush, charge it with pale ink, then add a small amount of burnt sienna. Use this for the birds' breasts. Complete the picture by adding touches of burnt sienna to the wings and eyes and yellow around the eyes.

Hydrangea

Prepare the base area of the flower in the following way. Select a medium tsuketate brush. With it prepare pale green by mixing viridian with white and charging a brush with this pigment in the usual gradations. Add a small amount of light cobalt blue. Blend these by making two or three zigzag strokes across the mixing dish. Then paint a large area like A in the model. To accomplish this you may have to prepare colors and recharge the brush a number of times. Do not attempt to cut labor by mixing a large quantity of color at once, because invariably such a practice leads to a flat, uninteresting color in the large painted zone. Though it is somewhat more time-demanding, mixing and charging afresh each time additional paint is needed produce a complicated, varied, hence, interesting color.

Using the same brush and without taking additional water, create a pale red by mixing carmine and white. Apply this in the upper right part of the blue zone so that the two overlap slightly. Next, once again preparing blue as described in the preceding paragraph but making the color slightly darker, overpaint from place to place to give depth and to prevent the color from being flat. Paint the hydrangea leaves before adding the flower outlines.

Whether you are dealing with color or with ink, the charging of the brush must carefully follow the procedures outlined on p. 22. In painting the hydrangea leaves, first wash a tsuketate brush in water. Charge it with pale ink in such a way that the base of the bristles remain filled with nothing but clear water. Add dark ink to about one-third the length of the bristles and blend by making two or three zigzag strokes across the surface of the mixing dish. Begin with the large, dark leaves. To prevent the sudden appearance of an unwanted dark zone, attempt to cover as many of the leaves as possible with a single brush. Then add modula-

tion and tonal variation as required. If the paper you are using is highly absorbent, you may overpaint while the first coat is still wet.

Returning to the flowers, add the petals with a line brush, taking care to vary the color of the lines to suit variations in the base color. Emphasize the centers by dipping only the tip of the brush in indigo and applying it to the paper without mixing.

The veins in the leaves must be added in two stages: while the base ink is wet for the paler leaves and after the base has dried for the stronger, darker ones. Adjust your brushwork to ensure that the veins are not fragile in appearance. **35**

Turtledove

To make the color for the head at step 4, mix white with carmine
and cerulean blue. Intensify the cerulean blue in the mixture for the
color of the back (step 5) and add more carmine for the breast.
Using another brush, make the feather markings (step 6) with
burnt sienna or light red. The pinions (step 7) are made with a
slender side stroke, with the handle of the brush slightly inclined.
The tail feathers are made with a half-side stroke in which the
handle of the brush is only slightly inclined. Branches near the
trunk are made with two strokes.

For the flowers, charge the brush with cobalt blue, add a small amount of indigo to the tip of the brush, and blend lightly.

Iris

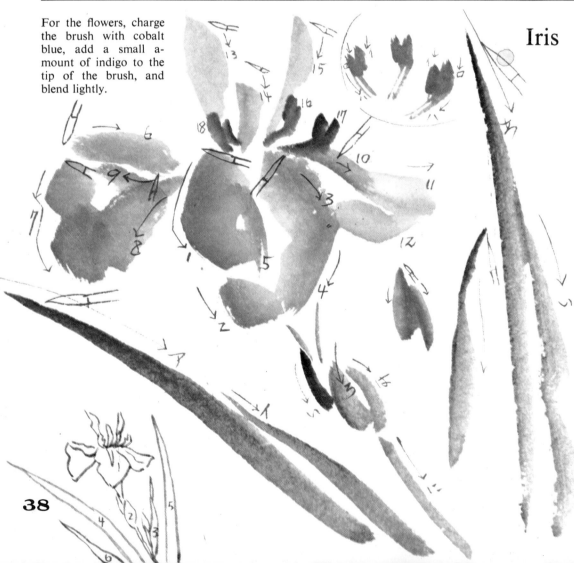

38

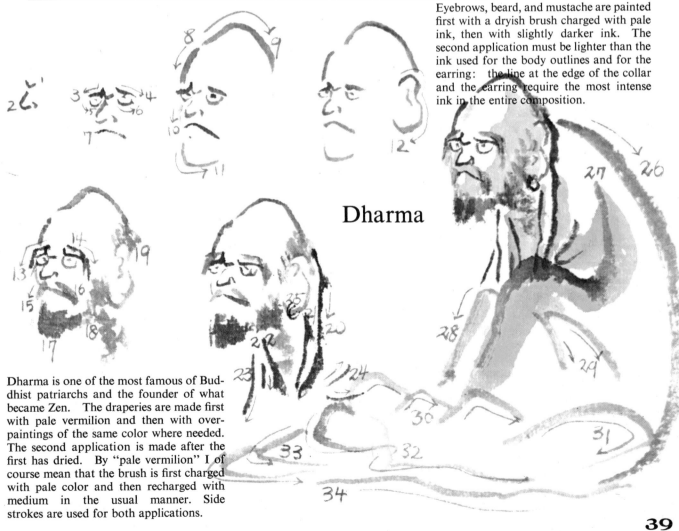

Eyebrows, beard, and mustache are painted first with a dryish brush charged with pale ink, then with slightly darker ink. The second application must be lighter than the ink used for the body outlines and for the earring: the line at the edge of the collar and the earring require the most intense ink in the entire composition.

Dharma

Dharma is one of the most famous of Buddhist patriarchs and the founder of what became Zen. The draperies are made first with pale vermilion and then with over-paintings of the same color where needed. The second application is made after the first has dried. By "pale vermilion" I of course mean that the brush is first charged with pale color and then recharged with medium in the usual manner. Side strokes are used for both applications.

39

Bird

Although the circle around the bird's eye seems pure white, in fact it must be painted with a brush charged with three tones of ink. A small tsuketate brush is good for this picture, but a handmade line brush too will give adequate stroke widths. The brushwork used in the feathers at steps 7 and 8 is exactly like that used for the plumage of the herons (p. 32). Use side strokes for most of the feathers, but in the tail, half-side strokes are necessary. Move the brush toward you in a continuous, unbroken movement that begins before the brush touches paper and continues into the air a few inches after the brush has been lifted. Begin the branch with a half-side stroke but gradually lift the handle upward until you are using a vertical stroke for the slender twigs at the end. For the foliage, charge the brush with pale burnt sienna, add very small quantities of carmine and indigo to the tip of the bristles, and, after mixing lightly, paint the leaves. The resulting color will be a faintly purplish brown. It is best to paint the bird's leg and foot after the branch is finished. Even so, to ensure an appearance of stability in the bird's body and accurate placement of the foot, establish the position of the branch on the paper and indicate it lightly with charcoal at the very outset.

Chrysanthemums and Sparrow

42

Begin the line drawing for the chrysanthemum petals on the lower left side of each blossom and draw the petals in numerical order. Vary the petals as they are uninteresting if too regularly placed. For the color in the petals, first charge the brush with carmine to which a small quantity of indigo (or cobalt blue) has been added. The first application must be pale; when this dries, intensity may be added where needed by overpainting. Be sure to charge the color brush and the ink brushes in the standard three-tone fashion.

Begin painting the leaves with 4, 5, and 6, which are darker and stronger, then move on to the paler ones. Paint all the leaves once; while they are still wet, go back to each and darken the centers by overpainting.

The color for the upper parts of the body of the sparrow is somewhat complicated. First charge a handmade line brush with a mixture of yellow ochre and burnt sienna. Blend this by making four or five zigzag strokes over the surface of the mixing dish. To the tip of the bristles, add small quantities of carmine and indigo. Finally, take a very small quantity of ink on the tip from a part of a mixing dish where the ink has already dried. Blend again in a mixing dish, then apply to paper.

Morning Glories

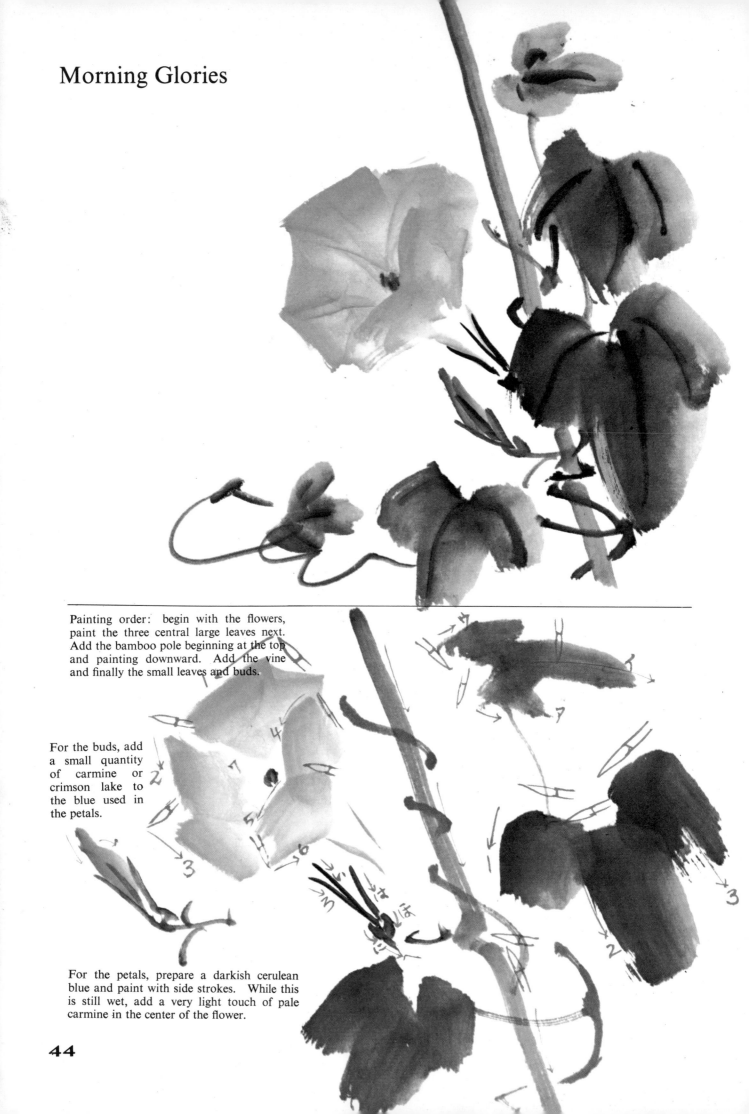

Painting order: begin with the flowers, paint the three central large leaves next. Add the bamboo pole beginning at the top and painting downward. Add the vine and finally the small leaves and buds.

For the buds, add a small quantity of carmine or crimson lake to the blue used in the petals.

For the petals, prepare a darkish cerulean blue and paint with side strokes. While this is still wet, add a very light touch of pale carmine in the center of the flower.

44

Cat and Narcissus

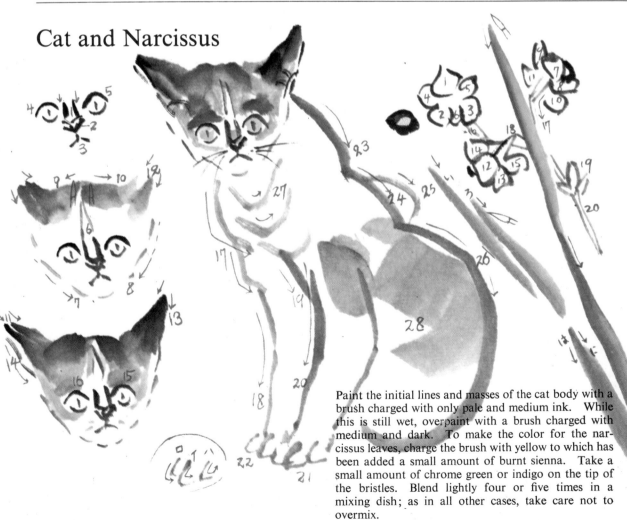

Paint the initial lines and masses of the cat body with a brush charged with only pale and medium ink. While this is still wet, overpaint with a brush charged with medium and dark. To make the color for the narcissus leaves, charge the brush with yellow to which has been added a small amount of burnt sienna. Take a small amount of chrome green or indigo on the tip of the bristles. Blend lightly four or five times in a mixing dish; as in all other cases, take care not to overmix.

Mountain Scene

Step 1: The scene represents the mountain in early summer when young greenery is still fresh and bright. Begin painting with the cloud masses; for these use a menso brush charged with water, pale, and medium ink. Use the same brush to add the outlines of the hills in the middle distance.

Charge a small tsuketate brush with pale, medium, and dark ink to paint in the trees. Use side strokes for these and move from the central darker forest mass gradually to the right. When the darker right portions of the tress have been finished, move to the left forest mass, which is generally lighter in tone. Add the pale ink lines in the foreground.

When it is necessary to recharge the brush, apply the first few strokes, which are naturally darker at some place where heavier tones are desired.

Step 2: Using a line brush, begin painting the right and left sides of the mountain at the top then move to the lower left outlines. Adding dark ink to the brush, paint some generous detail lines in the zone from the pinnacle to the middle part of the mountain. When you have completed the general mountain mass, charge a small tsuketate brush with relatively pale ink and after filling in the major zones of the mountain, move to the smaller hills

in the middle ground and to the trees. Next paint the clouds, taking care to give them abundance without allowing them to seem as rigid and hard as the mountain. In specifying relatively pale ink in the this step, I mean a brush filled with water, pale, and middle ink.

Step 3: Charge a brush with pale yellow ochre to which has been added a small amount of burnt sienna. Use this color to paint the lower forested part of the mountain, the middle ground, the houses, and part of the lower forests and fields.

Moonlit Fishing Village

Step 1: Since the composition of this picture of a fishing village is somewhat complicated, indicate the general locations of objects with charcoal before beginning painting. There is no need to draw in details; the amount of sketching shown in Step 1 is sufficient. It will not be necessary to erase the charcoal lines.

Step 2: First charge a brush with a slightly pale version of the standard three-tone ink then add further pale ink to about half the length of the bristles. Begin by painting the roofs of the houses

and work over the whole composition. Use a brushwork technique somewhere between drawing and painting. Leave the circle of the moon untouched, but paint around it to achieve a soft effect.

Step 3: While the palish ink applied in step 2 is still wet, add darker lines beginning with the two-story house in the center of the picure. As I have said before, for line drawings, charge the brush with pale ink, press out most of the moisture, then add dark ink to the tip of the bristles. Blend with two or three strokes over the surface of the mixing dish. Make broad lines with a small choryu brush to indicate forests on the mountains in the back-

ground. Overpaint with pale ink in the zones that are shaded by the roof and in the streets. In order to achieve the desired stroke in which one side is blurred and softer than the other, wash the brush, charge the bristles about one-third full of pale ink, and use side strokes.

Step 4: Allow the ink to dry well. Paint the roofs and roads with pale cobalt. In another brush, prepare pale burnt sienna to which a very small quantity of ink has been added. Use this to touch up walls of buildings. In preparing this kind of lightly colored mixture, always wash the brush and take only enough color to extend to about one-sixth or one-seventh of the length of the bristles.

49

Praying Mantis and Crepe Myrtle

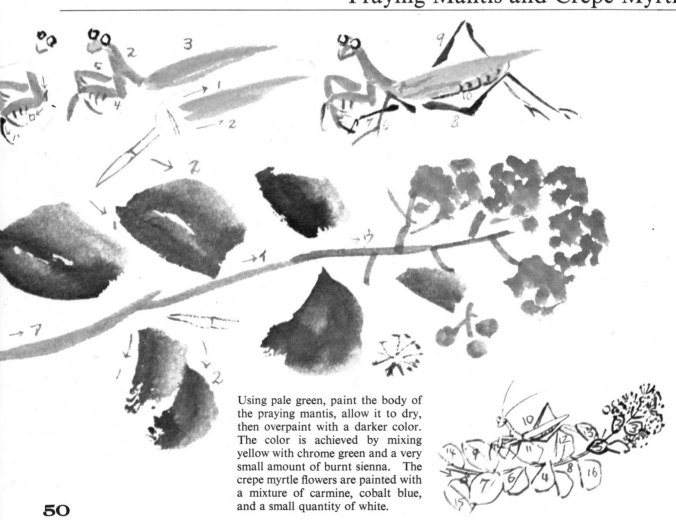

Using pale green, paint the body of the praying mantis, allow it to dry, then overpaint with a darker color. The color is achieved by mixing yellow with chrome green and a very small amount of burnt sienna. The crepe myrtle flowers are painted with a mixture of carmine, cobalt blue, and a small quantity of white.

Squirrel

First paint the body of the squirrel with a mixture of pale burnt sienna and a small quantity of ink. When this has dried, overpaint back and head with a slightly darker version of the same color. While this is wet, add the stripes with a brush charged with pale and medium ink. After waiting a few minutes, overpaint the stripes as needed with a brush charged with medium and dark ink.

Begin the leaves with the darker central ones. While they are wet overpaint with darker ink. The branches must be slightly darker than the leaves. The darkest things in the picture must be the squirrel's eye and the line at the top of his eye. Keeping a careful watch on the entire composition, do not allow any other lines to attain the intensity of these two points. Using a mixture of white (in fairly high proportion) carmine, and a small amount of burnt sienna, paint the paws. Add the claws with ink while the paws are still wet.

51

Pomegranate and Bluebird

In this picture, the body form has been somewhat more abbreviated than it was in the preceding pictures of birds. Though the position of the foot may present some difficulty, it will be easier to paint if you make initial positioning marks with charcoal and if you turn the paper to a comfortable angle. A very small amount of ink is added to the yellow ochre and vermilion in the pomegranates themselves. Additions of carmine to one and indigo to the other pomegranate establish good contrast. The branch is painted with side strokes of a line brush. The leaves with single strokes of a tsuketate brush.

53

Rose Mallow

The petals are first painted with crimson lake to which a small amount of white has been added. The first coat is pale, and overpainting is applied while the first application of paint is wet. The amount of paint used is plentiful; consequently, the edges are blurred, but this contributes to a suc-cessfully soft appearance. In nature, the center of the rose mallow is red-purple, but darkish ink is used in the picture for the sake of contrast. A handmade line brush is satisfactory. Paint the veins in the leaves to look somewhat thick.

Chrysanthemums

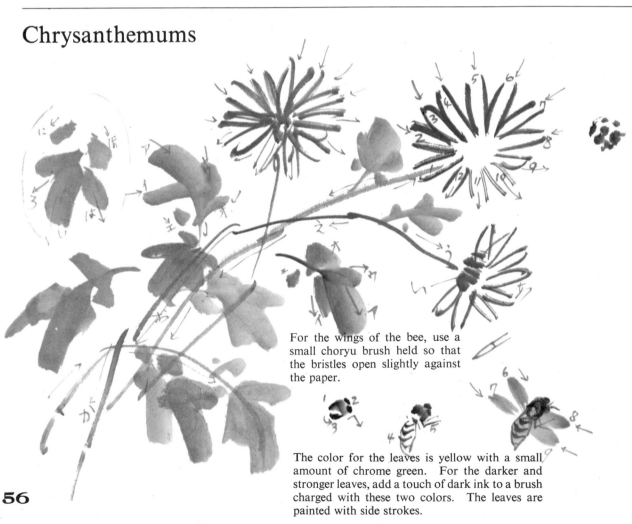

For the wings of the bee, use a small choryu brush held so that the bristles open slightly against the paper.

The color for the leaves is yellow with a small amount of chrome green. For the darker and stronger leaves, add a touch of dark ink to a brush charged with these two colors. The leaves are painted with side strokes.

Red Sea Snapper and Seashell

First draw the eye and outlines of the fish. Then, after charging a brush with correctly shaded vermilion, begin painting the colored parts. Start with the head. When the first application has dried, using a somewhat darker vermilion, add highlights and the fins.

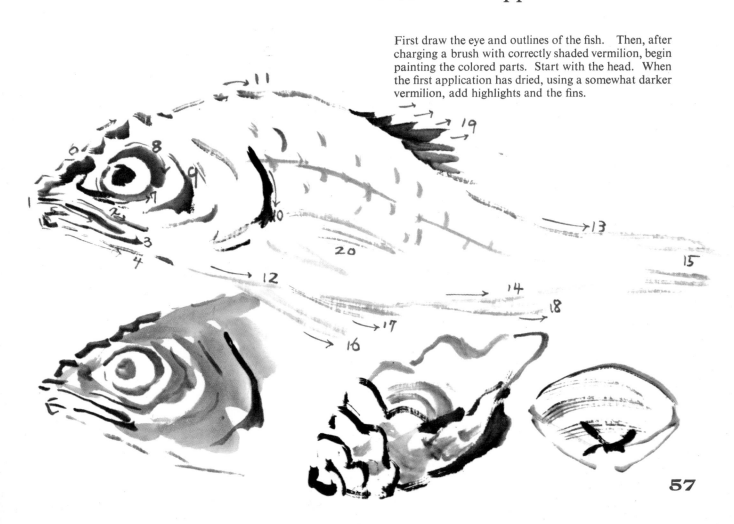

57

Peony

58

Charging a brush with three-tone carmine red, paint the petals. While this is wet, overpaint with a slightly darker carmine. While you allow the flower to dry, paint the stems and leaves. Using a menso or other small brush, paint the veins while the leaves are wet. When the flower is dry, add lines of ink in the center of the flower; paint the center at the same time. Then paint over the petals once more with carmine. Adding a light touch of the same carmine to the already painted leaves intensifies the beauty of the green.

Frog and Dragonfly

Since this picture is slightly impressionistic, I have used a color for the frog that would never occur in nature; still this kind of departure sometimes has interesting results. It is not as easy to be completely abstract as might seem to be the case. In this instance, the effect of abstraction is achieved by limiting the number of strokes to a minimum, even in such details as the rock. To paint the frog's body, use a very thin indigo. Allow this to dry then over-paint with a slightly darker indigo. The brushes should be charged in such a way as to produce a certain amount of shading. Since the body of the dragonfly is slender, overpainting will result in blur-ring and an unpleasant thickening. It therefore must be avoided in the body, though touching up flat, uninteresting areas in the wings is possible.

Water Lilies

Using a medium choryu brush charged with pale and medium ink, paint the lily pads with generous strokes. While they are still wet, charging a brush with medium and dark ink, press out most of the moisture, and overpaint the leaves. In both cases, the brush must be charged with water and pale ink in the usual manner.

The flower and bud are painted with line brushes, but before doing that make a few strokes with pale blue as shown in the finished picture. If you add the ink outlines while the blue is still wet, you will achieve a pleasingly soft effect.

Camellias

First using a slightly pale color and side strokes, paint the general shapes of the flowers. Then go over both with a slightly darker red. While the flowers are wet, add the ink lines. When they have dried, touch the deep parts of the flowers with darker red. Brush in the leaves with pale and medium ink first then go over them with medium and dark ink. Overpaint with dark ink another time on the larger, strong leaves. Blurring at the edges will only enhance the effect.

63

Java Sparrow and Quince

A handmade line brush should be sufficient for the bird. To paint the beak outlines, you must charge a brush with pale ink, press almost all of the moisture out, then dip the bristles into darker ink. Unless you follow this procedure, the lines of the beak and head will not be as beautiful as they ought to be. To make the gray-blue of the body, add white to indigo, mix, then add pale ink. In order to avoid flat colors, even in such small parts as the beak, overpaint. At steps 7 and 8, the gray has been intensified with slightly darker ink before overpainting. Paint the wings and tail as for the other bird pictures.

To make the color for the bird's breast, wash the brush, charge it with water, thin the remaining gray-blue in the mixing dish, and add a small amount of burnt sienna to the brush. The flower color is achieved by adding a very small smount of chrome green to yellow. White is added to prevent blurring. For the leaves, charge a brush with yellow. Add a little burnt sienna and a small amount of indigo. Blend by making five or six strokes across the surface of the mixing dish. First paint all the leaves then, paying attention to balance and contrast, overpaint. Paint the leaf veins with ink while the leaves are still wet.

1

2

3

4

Landscape

The following two pictures are modernized versions of what is called Southern-style painting, which originated in China and became very popular in Japan. Though the brushwork in these pictures is like. that used in true Southern-style painting, these modern versions are more natural in general appearance. The dark trees are painted with a brush that has been charged with pale ink and then amply filled with dark ink. The brush, dark side forward, is pressed against the mixing dish so that the bristles spread. It is then applied in a pushing fashion to the paper. When lifting it from the pa-

per, pull it very slightly forward to make the stroke broader. Trees in the foreground may be painted with larger, vigorous strokes, but those in the upper part require finer work. It will be necessary to recharge the brush about three times. Use a menso or line brush to paint the trunks and branches of the willows. The green for the willows is made by mixing indigo and yellow. Blend by making four or five zigzag strokes across the mixing dish. Do not try to use the greens found in watercolor sets; this may save time, but the results will be inferior.

1

2

3

4

Mountain Scene with Temple

Lift this side slightly from the paper.

Press the dark side firmly against the paper.

68

This picture shows a modern use of a painting style developed by the Sung-period Chinese poet and artist Mi Fei. This method is used to indicate the foliage on the mountains and around the temple.

Charge a small tsuketate brush with pale ink. Sketch in the outlines in step 1 with a line brush. Begin with the hillocks in the foreground then start the mountain at 3 and 4, which are in about the middle of the mass. From there, move upward and then to the more distant mountains on the left.

In step 2, it becomes necessary to master the Mi Fei method of landscape painting. A small tsuketate brush is charged with pale ink then filled with dark ink. Spread the bristles of the tip by making zigzag strokes across the mixing dish. Without adjusting the bristles, but twisting the brush slightly forward, bring it to the paper. As the lower block on the preceding page shows, the bristles are held with the front side—the side charged with darker ink—pressed firmly against the paper. The rear side of the bristles is lifted slightly from the paper. Pressing the brush in this way makes an elongated dot like the ones shown on p. 69. Continue making more of these dots first on the left then on the right. They must not all be of the same size, and they must neither overlap regularly like brickwork or form regular stairstep lines. After having made darker dots of this kind in the foreground, move to the mountains.

Boulders

It is important that boulders do not seem flat. To give appropriate projections and and recessions in surfaces, avoid curved lines.

In strong lines, the gradual exhausting of the ink in the brush allows the creation of these important rough lines.

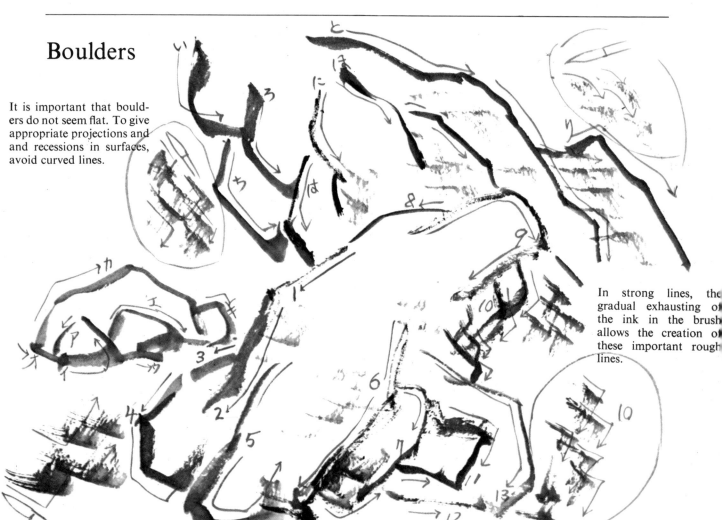

These apparently effortless lines help preserve rhythmical movement and give surface textures to rocks.

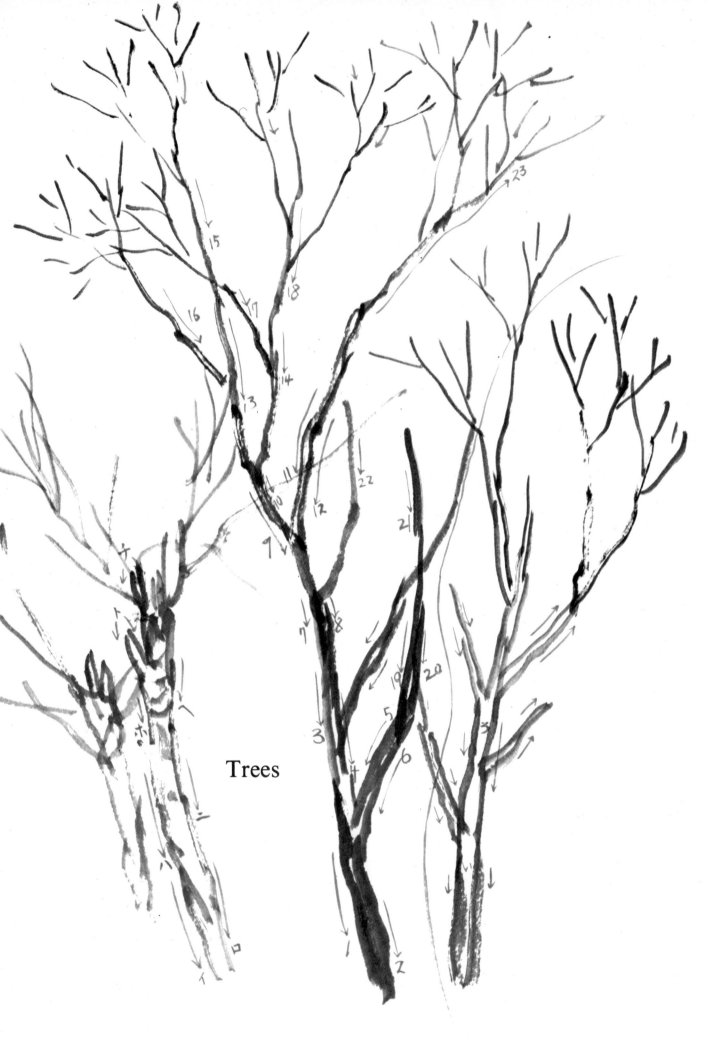

Trees

Sparrow and Bamboo

The examples of birds on pp. 42 and 64 should be sufficient explanation to enable you to paint this sparrow. The most troublesome parts are the head and wing. At step 6, if you use a half-side stroke, you will be able to achieve adequate width and good shading. To paint the fairly slender lines of the wing, incline the brush handle slightly to make side strokes. In general, a line brush is sufficient for most of the parts of the bird's body except the breast. In painting this part, a tsuketate brush will produce the required softness. To prepare the color for the bird's back, charge a brush with yellow ochre and burnt sienna, mix this by making five or six zigzag strokes on the mixing dish, take small quantities of carmine and indigo on the tip of the brush, and then a small quantity of medium ink. Blend with two or three zigzag strokes on the mixing dish.

The bamboo leaves are painted with side strokes of a small tsuketate brush. The brush must move through the air for one or two inches before it touches the paper, but press it against the paper firmly at the first part of each stroke.

Long-armed Ape

First establish the general position of the ape's body by making a light charcoal sketch of the two major ovals—body and head—of which the figure is composed. The left arm passes almost directly through the body oval. Once these three elements have been set, the right arm may be added. A straight line connecting the end of the right hand with the shoulder should form about a fifty-degree angle. Use a line brush for the nose, mouth, ears, and eyes and either line or tsuketate brush for the shaggy coat. As pure black paws would seem strange, paint them first with a pale ink, and then overpaint with dark ink. The coat is painted first with a brush charged with yellow ochre and burnt sienna. Overpainting is done with the same brush to which pale ink has been added. The branch is a combination of two lines made with a line brush. The vines are made with a small or medium menso brush; after they have been painted with medium ink, they require overpainting with darker ink. The dried leaves are made with a combination of yellow ochre, burnt sienna, and carmine. Use a small tsuketate brush. Produce the desired width by twisting the brush slightly to the side or the upper right just before lifting it from the paper.

Dried Lotus and Kingfisher

Once again, the bird is painted in a manner like that used for other similar subjects (pp. 42 and 73). Before adding the blue of the head, make a few strokes with an almost dry brush charged with pale ink (step 3). The natural kingfisher is so brilliantly colored that the Japanese sometimes call it the jade bird. But for the sake of this kind of painting, it is best to soften the colors for total harmony with the other elements of the composition. This effect is achieved by means of the use of small quantities of pale ink mixed with the other colors.

For the head use cobalt blue with a small amount of emerald green and white and a little pale ink. For the back, increase the amount of emerald green in the brush for the breast and belly, use carmine with a small amount of either cobalt blue or indigo. The dried lotus leaves are painted with a large tsuketate brush charged with yellow ochre, burnt sienna, and a small amount of ink. While they are still wet, charge a brush with the same colors, press out most of the moisture, then take—in this order—burnt sienna, carmine, and indigo into the brush. Blend to form a dark purplish color. Overpaint about one-third of the surface of the leaves with this color. Allow the leaves to dry slightly while you add the stems with a line brush. When they are finished, paint the veins on the leaves.

1

2

3

4

Seaside Scene

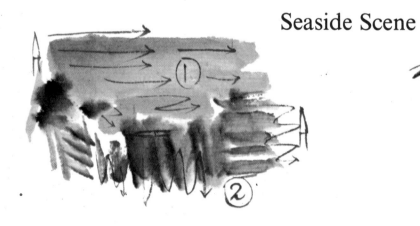

Step 1: After charging a small tsuketate brush with yellow ochre and burnt sienna, take a small amount of pale ink on the tip of the bristles. With side strokes, paint the roof of the shed in the foreground, then that of the shed in the background. Using the same brush take first pale then medium ink into the bristles; blend with two or three zigzag strokes over the mixing dish. Use this brush to add the weatherboards on the two buildings; paint those on the shed in the foreground first. Leave some blank areas among the strokes.

Step 2: With a tsuketate and a line brush, sketch in the mountains and buildings in the background and the fisherman who highlights the foreground.

Step 3: Charge a brush with chrome green; add a small quantity of emerald green to the tip. Blend well. Use this color to paint the water of the sea, taking care to leave unpainted areas to suggest whitecaps. For the mountain in the background, charge a brush with yellow ochre and burnt sienna, add a small amount of chrome green and blend by making four or five large zigzag strokes on the mixing dish. Paint in the mountain surfaces with this color. If the paper does not blot readily, you may overpaint while the first coat is still wet, but you must allow the initial application to dry if the paper is of the highly blotting variety. Paint the grasses in the foreground at this time.

Oleander

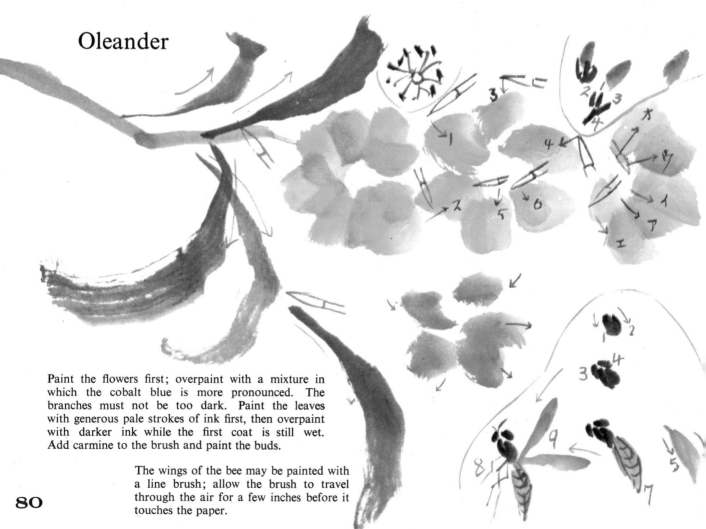

Paint the flowers first; overpaint with a mixture in which the cobalt blue is more pronounced. The branches must not be too dark. Paint the leaves with generous pale strokes of ink first, then overpaint with darker ink while the first coat is still wet. Add carmine to the brush and paint the buds.

The wings of the bee may be painted with a line brush; allow the brush to travel through the air for a few inches before it touches the paper.

Cow

Dancers at the Festival of the Lights

Because of the detail of the picture, this version of the dancers at the summer Festival of the Lights looks difficult. If you maintain correct proportional relations among head, body, and limbs, however, it is relatively simple to sketch in the line work and fill in the colors. The important thing is not the details, but the total feeling of movement. Drawing the dancers from life is difficult because they are constantly moving. One must therefore recall movements and attempt to combine recollections into a picture that captures the mood of the dance. This is true of pictures of moving animals as well. Of course, it is possible to resort to photographs for body position and other details. But since the human eye and the camera lens view things in completely different ways, this is not necessarily a good idea. For example, the mountain

view that the eye and the brain interpret in an emotional way is registered in the camera as no more than topographical features of certain shapes and sizes. The emotional attributes that make a picture impressive are missing and cannot be reconstituted on the basis of photographs alone.

In this picture the relationship between the heads and the feet are of special importance. Great care must be taken with the position of the foot on which the body weight rests: if it is too far forward or backward, the body will loose its appearance of stability. After drawing the face, im-

mediately determine the position in which the foot will produce a feeling of maximum balance. Remember that, in general, the head of a human figure is one-sixth as long as the entire figure.

When you have finished the details of the figures and their costumes, make a few strokes across the top of the background with a brush charged with greatly thinned vermilion. Next, with a medium tsuketate brush, charged with correctly shaded ink, make several bold, rough background strokes. Allow the paper to dry, then fill in with a smaller brush charged with shaded ink.

Grapes

Using a darker ink, paint the centers of the leaves while the outer parts are still wet. A small amount of white was added to both the first and second coats.

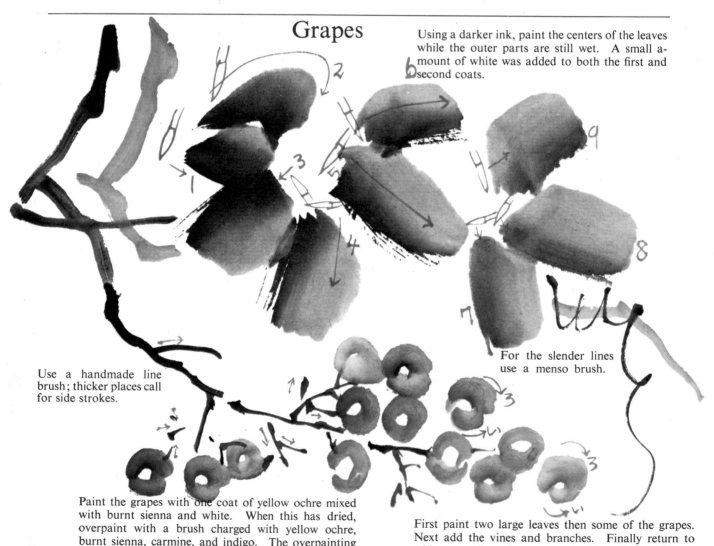

Use a handmade line brush; thicker places call for side strokes.

For the slender lines use a menso brush.

Paint the grapes with one coat of yellow ochre mixed with burnt sienna and white. When this has dried, overpaint with a brush charged with yellow ochre, burnt sienna, carmine, and indigo. The overpainting should be slightly farther toward the middle of each grape.

First paint two large leaves then some of the grapes. Next add the vines and branches. Finally return to add grapes where they are required for a balanced composition.

84

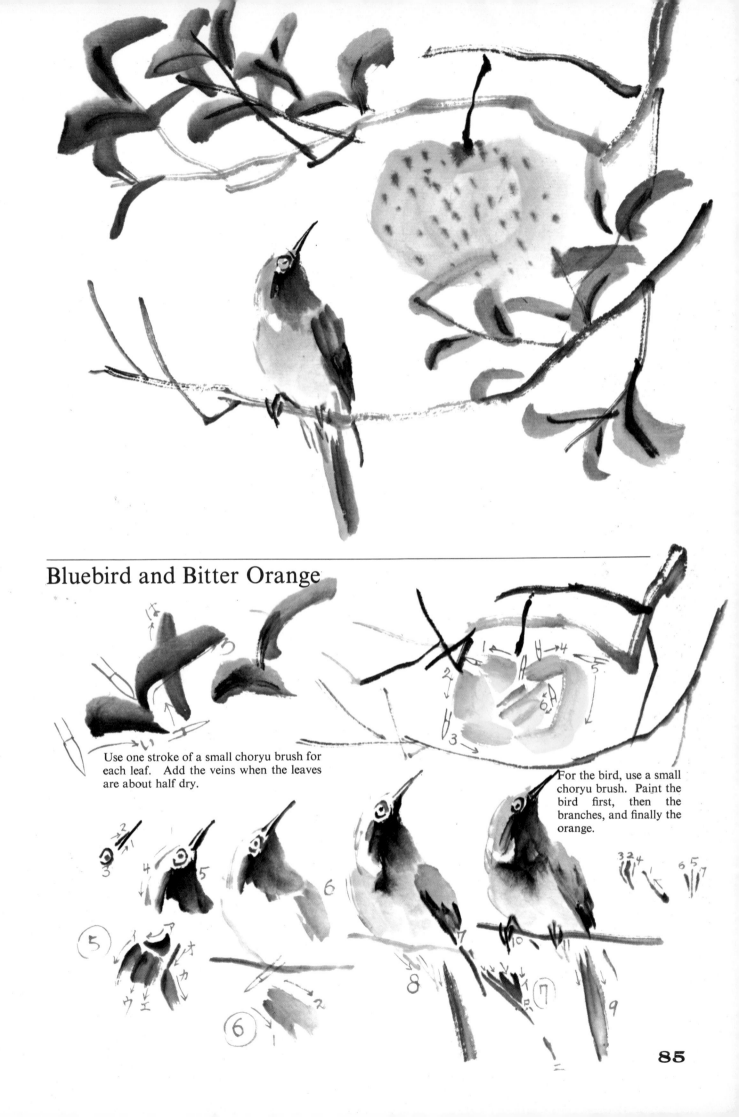

Bluebird and Bitter Orange

Use one stroke of a small choryu brush for each leaf. Add the veins when the leaves are about half dry.

For the bird, use a small choryu brush. Paint the bird first, then the branches, and finally the orange.

Sparrow and Plum

86

Even when the bird is facing directly forward, the order in painting does not vary from that already explained (see p. 40). For the large plum branches use either a line brush or a tsuketate brush, but you must use a line brush only for the slender twigs. Use a straight stroke for the latter and a side stroke for the former. When the first coat of ink on the thick branch has dried, overpaint with darker ink. The outlines of the flowers must be painted with a brush charged with pale ink and then dipped lightly into medium ink. The calyxes are painted with yellow to which a small amount of green has been added. The tip of the brush is then dipped into strong burnt sienna. Replenish the burnt sienna in the brush when it becomes thin.

Farm in the Mountains
in Autumn

88

Step 1: This picture was executed on paper with very low blotting characteristics. Since there are many details and since the composition is somewhat crowded, it is wise to make a detailed charcoal sketch before beginning painting. First sketch in the figure in the foreground, then the hayrick on the left, then the house in the middle, and finally the corner of a thatched roof on the right. Next move to the trees and finally to the mountains in the background.

Step 2: Using a brush charged with pale and medium ink, make overpainting strokes on the mountains, the roofs and the grasses in the fore-ground.

Step 3: In this step color is added. For the mountains, use yellow ochre and a small amount of burnt sienna. Lightly blend this in the mixing dish. Apply it with large bold strokes, and while it is still wet, overpaint with the same brush, after having added a small amount of vermilion and burnt sienna to the tip. Do not overblend. The two applications of color must blend softly while remaining clearly discernible. The autumn foliage on the trees immediately behind the farmhouse must be painted first with lighter color, allowed to dry, then overpainted with darker color.

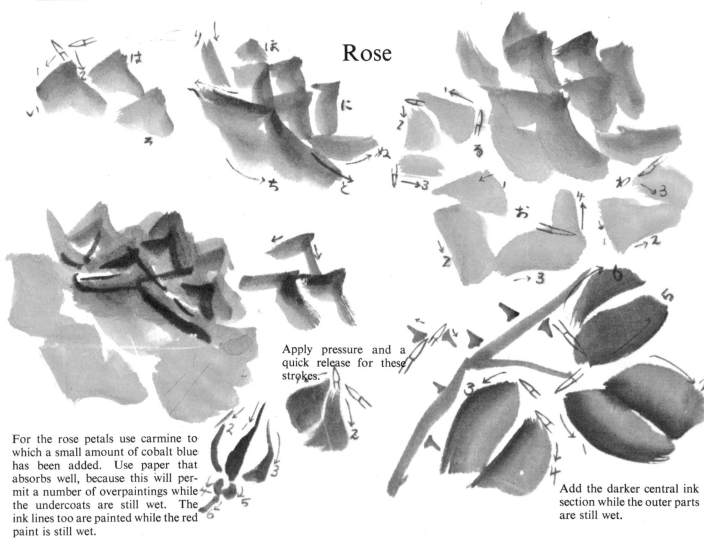

Rose

Apply pressure and a quick release for these strokes.

For the rose petals use carmine to which a small amount of cobalt blue has been added. Use paper that absorbs well, because this will permit a number of overpaintings while the undercoats are still wet. The ink lines too are painted while the red paint is still wet.

Add the darker central ink section while the outer parts are still wet.

Wild Duck in Reeds

For the wing plumage, paint these lines first with medium ink. Allow them to dry, then overpaint with a brush charged with medium and dark ink.

If these lines indicating breast plumage are painted while the undercoat is still wet, they will have a pleasing soft appearance.

For the overpainting use the same colors but increase the amount of pale ink.

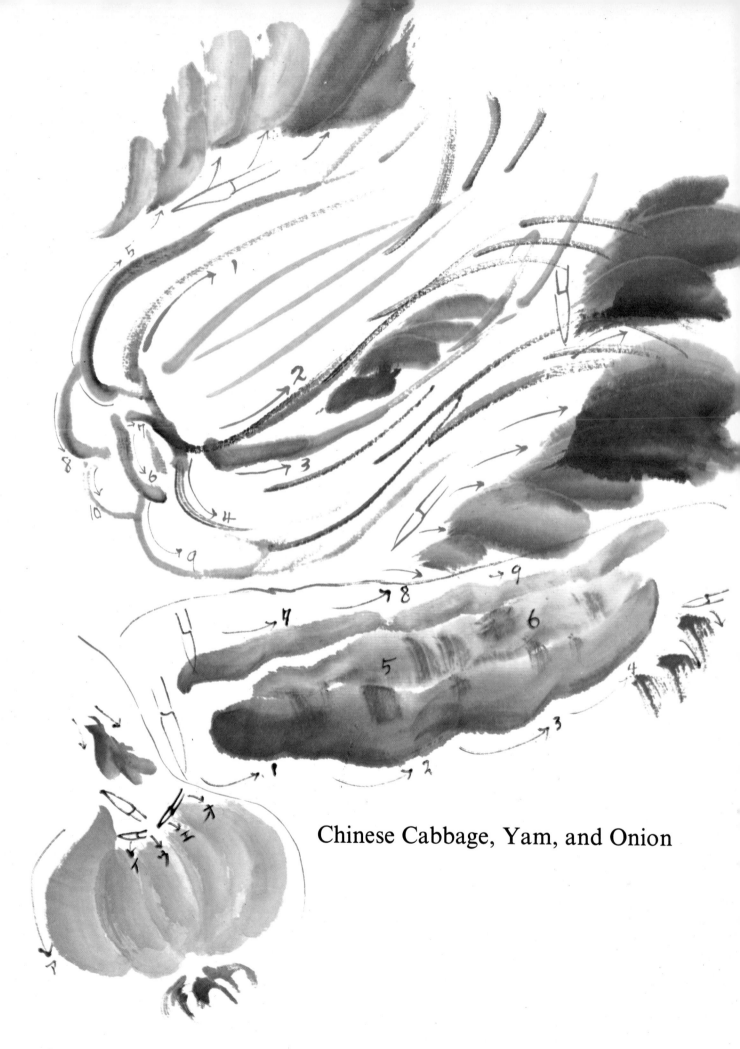

Chinese Cabbage, Yam, and Onion

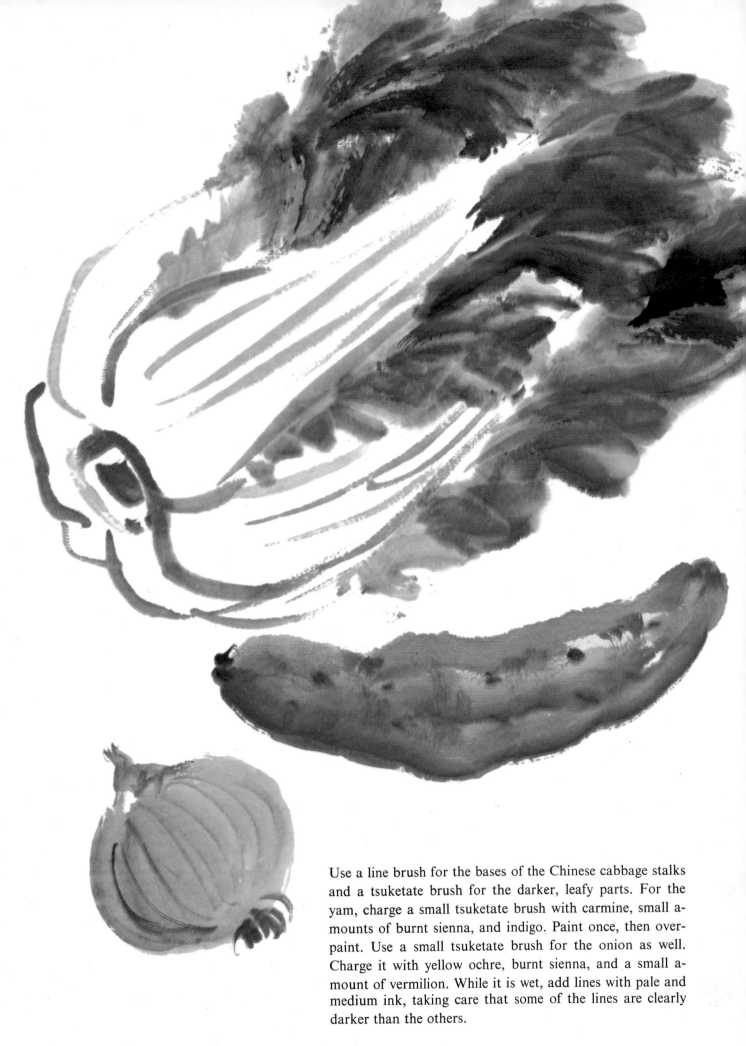

Use a line brush for the bases of the Chinese cabbage stalks and a tsuketate brush for the darker, leafy parts. For the yam, charge a small tsuketate brush with carmine, small amounts of burnt sienna, and indigo. Paint once, then overpaint. Use a small tsuketate brush for the onion as well. Charge it with yellow ochre, burnt sienna, and a small amount of vermilion. While it is wet, add lines with pale and medium ink, taking care that some of the lines are clearly darker than the others.

Paintings for Reference and Study

95

103